GOD'S TRUE
NATURE
Scriptural Devotional

GOD'S TRUE
NATURE

Scriptural Devotional

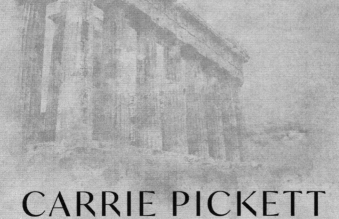

CARRIE PICKETT

Published in partnership between
Andrew Wommack Ministries and Harrison House Publishers

Shippensburg, PA 17257

ISBN 13 TP: 978-1-6675-0356-1

ISBN 13 eBook: 978-1-6675-0357-8

For Worldwide Distribution, Printed in the U.S.A.

1 2 3 4 5 6 7 8 / 27 26 25 24 23

Dedication:

May you always be drawn by the goodness of your God–so you can declare His love to the world.

Contents

Foreword

There is an attack on God's true nature. The enemy's goal is to deceive both believers and the world to think God is a harsh, distant, disappointed dictator toward them. The truth of who God really is can change our lives forever. The depths of His goodness and nature are contained in the Word of God.

In every single promise we see in the Word, we see the nature and character of God revealed. When you begin to see who He declares Himself to be in scripture, you realize that the promises are a direct reflection of His heart and mind toward you and how He wants to move and direct your life.

Through the promises of God, we've been equipped to know Him and invited to participate in His divine nature. With that invitation, we can enter into a higher level of relationship, power, and confidence of who God really is toward us.

Through this bold confidence of knowing our God, we can know who He is within us! God Almighty in

His fullness has made us His dwelling place. The fullness of the godhead living within our lives! What an amazing gift from God, that He doesn't hide Himself from us. We can fully know Him because He has placed His Word as the standard of how He operates.

This Scriptural Devotional is a starting point in discovering what the Word declares God to be and who He is. Throughout this Scriptural Devotional we have matched many of God's promises to His name. Participate in finding more verses and promises God shows you as you read the Word.

It is only through relationship with the Word that you can discover who God really is and how you've been invited to participate in the goodness and greatness of God.

Enjoy discovering even greater revelation of your God and His promises over you!

Blessings,

GOD'S TRUE NATURE

2 Peter 1:4 KJV

Whereby are given unto us exceeding great and precious promises: that by these ye might be partakers of the divine nature, having escaped the corruption that is in the world through lust.

Jeremiah 9:23-24 NKJV

Thus says the Lord: "Let not the wise man glory in his wisdom, let not the mighty man glory in his might, nor let the rich man glory in his riches; But let him who glories glory in this, that he understands and knows Me, that I am the Lord, exercising lovingkindness, judgment, and righteousness in the earth. For in these I delight," says the Lord.

Romans 8:28 BSB

And we know that God works all things together for the good of those who love Him, who are called according to His purpose.

1 Samuel 16:7 KJV

But the Lord said unto Samuel, Look not on his countenance, or on the height of his stature; because I have refused him: for the Lord seeth not as man seeth; for man looketh on the outward appearance, but the Lord looketh on the heart.

John 14:9-11 NKJV

Jesus said to him, "Have I been with you so long, and yet you have not known Me, Philip? He who has seen Me has seen the Father; so how can you say, 'Show us the Father'? Do you not believe that I am in the Father, and the Father in Me? The words that I speak to you I do not speak on My own authority; but the Father who dwells in Me does the works. Believe Me that I am in the Father and the Father in Me, or else believe Me for the sake of the works themselves."

1 Corinthians 2:10 AMP

For God has unveiled them and revealed them to us through the [Holy] Spirit; for the Spirit searches all things [diligently], even [sounding and measuring] the [profound] depths of God [the divine counsels and things far beyond human understanding].

Colossians 1:9-10 AMP

For this reason, since the day we heard about it, we have not stopped praying for you, asking [specifically] that you may be filled with the knowledge of His will in all spiritual wisdom [with insight into His purposes], and in understanding [of spiritual things], so that you will walk in a manner worthy of the Lord [displaying admirable character, moral courage, and personal integrity], to [fully] please Him in all things, bearing fruit in every good work and steadily growing in the knowledge of God [with deeper faith, clearer insight and fervent love for His precepts].

John 3:16 NKJV

For God so loved the world that He gave His only begotten Son, that whoever believes in Him should not perish but have everlasting life.

1 Corinthians 2:11-12 KJV

For what man knoweth the things of a man, save the spirit of man which is in him? even so the things of God knoweth no man, but the Spirit of God. Now we have received, not the spirit of the world, but the spirit which is of God; that we might know the things that are freely given to us of God.

2 Corinthians 3:17 NIV

Now the Lord is the Spirit, and where the Spirit of the Lord is, there is freedom.

2 Peter 1:3-4 ESV

His divine power has granted to us all things that pertain to life and godliness, through the knowledge of him who called us to his own glory and excellence, by which he has granted to us his precious and very great promises, so that through them you may become partakers of the divine nature, having escaped from the corruption that is in the world because of sinful desire.

JEHOVAH

I AM the One Who Is the Self Existent One

Malachi 3:6 KJV

*For I am the Lord, I change not; therefore
ye sons of Jacob are not consumed.*

James 1: 17 AMP

Every good thing given and every perfect gift is from above; it comes down from the Father of lights [the Creator and Sustainer of the heavens], in whom there is no variation [no rising or setting] or shadow cast by His turning [for He is perfect and never changes].

Psalm 102:27 KJV

But thou art the same, and thy years shall have no end.

Psalm 136:7 BSB

He made the great lights—His loving devotion endures forever.

Malachi 3:6 AMP

For I am the Lord, I do not change [but remain faithful to My covenant with you]; that is why you, O sons of Jacob, have not come to an end.

Numbers 23:19-20 NLT

God is not a man, so he does not lie. He is not human, so he does not change his mind. Has he ever spoken and failed to act? Has he ever promised and not carried it through? Listen, I received a command to bless; God has blessed, and I cannot reverse it!

Lamentations 3:22 ESV

The steadfast love of the Lord never ceases; his mercies never come to an end.

Genesis 2:4 ESV

These are the generations of the heavens and the earth when they were created, in the day that the Lord God made the earth and the heavens.

Revelation 11:15 NKJV

Then the seventh angel sounded: And there were loud voices in heaven, saying, "The kingdoms of this world have become the kingdoms of our Lord and of His Christ, and He shall reign forever and ever!"

Deuteronomy 7:9 ESV

Know therefore that the Lord your God is God, the faithful God who keeps covenant and steadfast love with those who love him and keep his commandments, to a thousand generations.

Titus 1:2 NIV

In the hope of eternal life, which God, who does not lie, promised before the beginning of time.

1 Kings 8:56-59 NKJV

Blessed be the Lord, who has given rest to His people Israel, according to all that He promised. There has not failed one word of all His good promise, which He promised through His servant Moses. May the Lord our God be with us, as He was with our fathers. May He not leave us nor forsake us, that He may incline our hearts to Himself, to walk in all His ways, and to keep His commandments and His statutes and His judgments, which He commanded our fathers. And may these words of mine, with which I have made supplication before the Lord, be near the Lord our God day and night, that He may maintain the cause of His servant and the cause of His people Israel, as each day may require.

2 Timothy 2:13 NKJV

If we are faithless, He remains faithful; He cannot deny Himself.

1 Thessalonians 5:24 AMP

Faithful and absolutely trustworthy is He who is calling you [to Himself for your salvation], and He will do it [He will fulfill His call by making you holy, guarding you, watching over you, and protecting you as His own].

Genesis 28:15 AMP

Behold, I am with you and will keep [careful watch over you and guard] you wherever you may go, and I will bring you back to this [promised] land; for I will not leave you until I have done what I have promised you.

Joshua 21:45 BSB

Not one of all the LORD's good promises to the house of Israel had failed; everything was fulfilled.

Isaiah 48:3 KJV

I have declared the former things from the beginning; and they went forth out of my mouth, and I shewed them; I did them suddenly, and they came to pass.

Joshua 23:14 NKJV

Behold, this day I am going the way of all the earth. And you know in all your hearts and in all your souls that not one thing has failed of all the good things which the Lord your God spoke concerning you. All have come to pass for you; not one word of them has failed.

ELOHIM

The All Powerful One

Isaiah 54:5 NKJV

*For your Maker is your husband, the Lord of hosts
is His name; And your Redeemer is the Holy One of
Israel; He is called the God of the whole earth.*

Jeremiah 32:27 KJV

Behold, I am the Lord, the God of all flesh: is there any thing too hard for me?

Isaiah 6:3 NKJV

And one cried to another and said: "Holy, holy, holy is the Lord of hosts; The whole earth is full of His glory!"

Isaiah 11:9 ESV

They shall not hurt or destroy in all my holy mountain; for the earth shall be full of the knowledge of the Lord as the waters cover the sea.

Isaiah 45:11 ESV

Thus says the Lord, the Holy One of Israel, and the one who formed him: "Ask me of things to come; will you command me concerning my children and the work of my hands?"

Isaiah 51:15 NLT

For I am the Lord your God, who stirs up the sea, causing its waves to roar. My name is the Lord of Heaven's Armies.

Zechariah 14:9 NIV

The Lord will be king over the whole earth. On that day there will be one Lord, and his name the only name.

Jeremiah 32:17 AMP

Ah Lord God! Behold, You have made the heavens and the earth by Your great power and by Your outstretched arm! There is nothing too difficult or too wonderful for You.

Genesis 2:19 BSB

And out of the ground the LORD God formed every beast of the field and every bird of the air, and He brought them to the man to see what he would name each one. And whatever the man called each living creature, that was its name.

Psalm 60:5 NKJV

That Your beloved may be delivered, save with Your right hand, and hear me.

Deuteronomy 10:21 AMP

He is your praise and glory; He is your God, who has done for you these great and awesome things which you have seen with your own eyes.

Proverbs 29:25 BSB

The fear of man is a snare, but whoever trusts in the LORD is set securely on high.

Isaiah 25:8-9 BSB

He will swallow up death forever. The Lord GOD will wipe away the tears from every face and remove the disgrace of His people from the whole earth. For the LORD has spoken. And in that day it will be said, "Surely this is our God; we have waited for Him, and He has saved us. This is the LORD for whom we have waited. Let us rejoice and be glad in His salvation."

Psalm 27:1, 5-6 BSB

The LORD is my light and my salvation—whom shall I fear? The LORD is the stronghold of my life—whom shall I dread? For in the day of trouble He will hide me in His shelter; He will conceal me under the cover of His tent; He will set me high upon a rock. Then my head will be held high above my enemies around me. At His tabernacle I will offer sacrifices with shouts of joy; I will sing and make music to the LORD.

Isaiah 54:17 AMP

"No weapon that is formed against you will succeed; And every tongue that rises against you in judgment you will condemn. This [peace, righteousness, security, and triumph over opposition] is the heritage of the servants of the Lord, dnd this is their vindication from Me," says the Lord.

2 Timothy 1:7 NKJV

For God has not given us a spirit of fear, but of power and of love and of a sound mind.

Psalm 34:4 BSB

I sought the LORD, and He answered me; He delivered me from all my fears.

1 Corinthians 15:54 NKJV

So when this corruptible has put on incorruption, and this mortal has put on immortality, then shall be brought to pass the saying that is written: "Death is swallowed up in victory."

2 Timothy 1:10 AMP

But now [that extraordinary purpose and grace] has been fully disclosed and realized by us through the appearing of our Savior Christ Jesus who [through His incarnation and earthly ministry] abolished death [making it null and void] and brought life and immortality to light through the gospel.

Isaiah 45:24 NIV

They will say of me, "In the Lord alone are deliverance and strength." All who have raged against him will come to him and be put to shame.

Isaiah 61:11 AMP

For as the earth brings forth its sprouts, and as a garden causes what is sown in it to spring up, so the Lord God will [most certainly] cause righteousness and justice and praise to spring up before all the nations [through the power of His word].

Psalm 71:16-19 BSB

I will enter in the strength of the Lord GOD; I will proclaim Your righteousness—Yours alone. O God, You have taught me from my youth, and to this day I proclaim Your marvelous deeds. Even when I am old and gray, do not forsake me, O God, until I proclaim Your power to the next generation, Your might to all who are to come. Your righteousness reaches to the heavens, O God, You who have done great things. Who, O God, is like You?

Psalm 34:17-19 BSB

The righteous cry out, and the LORD hears; He delivers them from all their troubles. The LORD is near to the brokenhearted; He saves the contrite in spirit. Many are the afflictions of the righteous, but the LORD delivers him from them all.

EL-ROI

The God Who Sees Me

Jeremiah 29:11-14 ESV

*For I know the plans I have for you, declares the Lord,
plans for welfare and not for evil, to give you a future and
a hope. Then you will call upon me and come and pray
to me, and I will hear you. You will seek me and find me,
when you seek me with all your heart. I will be found by
you, declares the Lord, and I will restore your fortunes and
gather you from all the nations and all the places where
I have driven you, declares the Lord, and I will bring
you back to the place from which I sent you into exile.*

Jeremiah 30:10 ESV

Then fear not, O Jacob my servant, declares the Lord nor be dismayed, O Israel; for behold, I will save you from far away, and your offspring from the land of their captivity. Jacob shall return and have quiet and ease, and none shall make him afraid.

Isaiah 41:13 NIV

For I am the Lord your God who takes hold of your right hand and says to you, Do not fear; I will help you.

Isaiah 43:5 AMP

Do not fear, for I am with you; I will bring your offspring from the east [where they are scattered], and gather you from the west.

Genesis 15:1 KJV

After these things the word of the Lord came unto Abram in a vision, saying, Fear not, Abram: I am thy shield, and thy exceeding great reward.

Deuteronomy 31:6-8 AMP

"Be strong and courageous, do not be afraid or tremble in dread before them, for it is the Lord your God who goes with you. He will not fail you or abandon you." Then Moses called to Joshua and said to him in the sight of all [the people of] Israel, "Be strong and courageous, for you will go with this people into the land which the Lord has sworn to their fathers to give them, and you will give it to them as an inheritance. It is the Lord who goes before you; He will be with you. He will not fail you or abandon you. Do not fear or be dismayed."

Isaiah 41:10 KJV

Fear thou not; for I am with thee: be not dismayed; for I am thy God: I will strengthen thee; yea, I will help thee; yea, I will uphold thee with the right hand of my righteousness.

Isaiah 43:2 NKJV

When you pass through the waters, I will be with you; And through the rivers, they shall not overflow you. When you walk through the fire, you shall not be burned, nor shall the flame scorch you.

Psalm 23:4 AMP

Even though I walk through the [sunless] valley of the shadow of death, I fear no evil, for You are with me; Your rod [to protect] and Your staff [to guide], they comfort and console me.

Joshua 1:5 KJV

There shall not any man be able to stand before thee all the days of thy life: as I was with Moses, so I will be with thee: I will not fail thee, nor forsake thee.

Exodus 4:12 BSB

Now go! I will help you as you speak, and I will teach you what to say.

Jeremiah 7:23 NKJV

But this is what I commanded them, saying, "Obey My voice, and I will be your God, and you shall be My people. And walk in all the ways that I have commanded you, that it may be well with you."

Leviticus 26:11-12 BSB

And I will make My dwelling place among you, and My soul will not despise you. I will walk among you and be your God, and you will be My people.

Exodus 19:5 KJV

Now therefore, if ye will obey my voice indeed, and keep my covenant, then ye shall be a peculiar treasure unto me above all people: for all the earth is mine.

Psalm 103:17-18 ESV

But the steadfast love of the Lord is from everlasting to everlasting on those who fear him, and his righteousness to children's children, to those who keep his covenant and remember to do his commandments.

Deuteronomy 7:6 AMP

For you are a holy people [set apart] to the Lord your God; the Lord your God has chosen you out of all the peoples on the face of the earth to be a people for His own possession [that is, His very special treasure].

1 Peter 2:9-10 ESV

But you are a chosen race, a royal priesthood, a holy nation, a people for his own possession, that you may proclaim the excellencies of him who called you out of darkness into his marvelous light. Once you were not a people, but now you are God's people; once you had not received mercy, but now you have received mercy.

Titus 2:14 AMP

Who [willingly] gave Himself [to be crucified] on our behalf to redeem us and purchase our freedom from all wickedness, and to purify for Himself a chosen and very special people to be His own possession, who are enthusiastic for doing what is good.

Deuteronomy 26:18 BSB

And today the LORD has proclaimed that you are His people and treasured possession as He promised, that you are to keep all His commandments.

Psalm 17:8 AMP

Keep me [in Your affectionate care, protect me] as the apple of Your eye; Hide me in the [protective] shadow of Your wings.

Psalm 27:5-6 NKJV

For in the time of trouble He shall hide me in His pavilion; In the secret place of His tabernacle He shall hide me; He shall set me high upon a rock. And now my head shall be lifted up above my enemies all around me; Therefore I will offer sacrifices of joy in His tabernacle; I will sing, yes, I will sing praises to the Lord.

Psalm 57:1 NLT

Have mercy on me, O God, have mercy! I look to you for protection. I will hide beneath the shadow of your wings until the danger passes by.

Psalm 40:2 AMP

He brought me up out of a horrible pit [of tumult and of destruction], out of the miry clay, and He set my feet upon a rock, steadying my footsteps and establishing my path.

IMMANUEL

God With Us

Matthew 1:23 ESV

Behold, the virgin shall conceive and bear a son,
and they shall call his name Immanuel.

Isaiah 7:14 KJV

Therefore the Lord himself shall give you a sign; Behold, a virgin shall conceive, and bear a son, and shall call his name Immanuel.

Isaiah 8:9-10 BSB

Huddle together, O peoples, and be shattered; pay attention, all you distant lands; prepare for battle, and be shattered; prepare for battle, and be shattered! Devise a plan, but it will be thwarted; state a proposal, but it will not happen. For God is with us.

Matthew 1:23 ESV

Behold, the virgin shall conceive and bear a son, and they shall call his name Immanuel.

John 14:16-17 ESV

And I will ask the Father, and he will give you another Helper, to be with you forever, even the Spirit of truth, whom the world cannot receive, because it neither sees him nor knows him. You know him, for he dwells with you and will be in you.

Romans 8:31 NKJV

What then shall we say to these things? If God is for us, who can be against us?

Matthew 28:20 NKJV

"Teaching them to observe all things that I have commanded you; and lo, I am with you always, even to the end of the age." Amen.

Psalm 46:7, 11 AMP

The Lord of hosts is with us; The God of Jacob is our stronghold [our refuge, our high tower]. Selah.

Matthew 18:20 ESV

For where two or three are gathered in my name, there am I among them.

2 Kings 6:16 NKJV

So he answered, "Do not fear, for those who are with us are more than those who are with them."

Psalm 56:9 KJV

When I cry unto thee, then shall mine enemies turn back: this I know; for God is for me.

Psalm 118:6 AMP

The Lord is on my side; I will not fear. What can [mere] man do to me?

Isaiah 41:10 AMP

Do not fear [anything], for I am with you; Do not be afraid, for I am your God. I will strengthen you, be assured I will help you; I will certainly take hold of you with My righteous right hand [a hand of justice, of power, of victory, of salvation].

Numbers 14:9 ESV

Only do not rebel against the Lord. And do not fear the people of the land, for they are bread for us. Their protection is removed from them, and the Lord is with us; do not fear them.

Psalm 91:1-2 AMP

He who dwells in the shelter of the Most High Will remain secure and rest in the shadow of the Almighty [whose power no enemy can withstand]. I will say of the Lord, "He is my refuge and my fortress, My God, in whom I trust [with great confidence, and on whom I rely]!"

Psalm 121:5 NLT

The Lord himself watches over you! The Lord stands beside you as your protective shade.

Deuteronomy 7:21 NKJV

You shall not be terrified of them; for the Lord your God, the great and awesome God, is among you.

Psalm 27:5 KJV

For in the time of trouble he shall hide me in his pavilion: in the secret of his tabernacle shall he hide me; he shall set me up upon a rock.

Psalm 31:20 NKJV

You shall hide them in the secret place of Your presence From the plots of man; You shall keep them secretly in a pavilion From the strife of tongues.

Psalm 32:7 ESV

You are a hiding place for me; you preserve me from trouble; you surround me with shouts of deliverance. Selah

Psalm 90:1 BSB

Lord, You have been our dwelling place through all generations.

Psalm 119:114 NLT

You are my refuge and my shield your word is my source of hope.

Psalm 17:8 KJV

Keep me as the apple of the eye, hide me under the shadow of thy wings.

Psalm 36:7 NKJV

How precious is Your lovingkindness, O God! Therefore the children of men put their trust under the shadow of Your wings.

Deuteronomy 20:1 BSB

When you go out to war against your enemies and see horses, chariots, and an army larger than yours, do not be afraid of them; for the LORD your God, who brought you out of the land of Egypt, is with you.

Isaiah 41:13-14 NKJV

"For I, the Lord your God, will hold your right hand, Saying to you, 'Fear not, I will help you.' Fear not, you worm Jacob, You men of Israel! I will help you," says the Lord And your Redeemer, the Holy One of Israel.

Isaiah 43:1, 5 BSB

Now this is what the LORD says—He who created you, O Jacob, and He who formed you, O Israel: "Do not fear, for I have redeemed you; I have called you by your name; you are Mine! ...Do not be afraid, for I am with you; I will bring your offspring from the east and gather you from the west."

Psalm 41:12 ESV

But you have upheld me because of my integrity, and set me in your presence forever.

JEHOVAH JIREH

The Lord Our Provider
Jehovah's Provision Will Be Seen

Genesis 22:14 NKJV

And Abraham called the name of the place, The-Lord-Will-Provide; as it is said to this day, "In the Mount of the Lord it shall be provided."

Philippians 4:19 AMP

And my God will liberally supply (fill until full) your every need according to His riches in glory in Christ Jesus.

Matthew 7:7-11 NIV

Ask and it will be given to you; seek and you will find; knock and the door will be opened to you. For everyone who asks receives; the one who seeks finds; and to the one who knocks, the door will be opened. Which of you, if your son asks for bread, will give him a stone? Or if he asks for a fish, will give him a snake? If you, then, though you are evil, know how to give good gifts to your children, how much more will your Father in heaven give good gifts to those who ask him!

Isaiah 30:23 NKJV

Then He will give the rain for your seed with which you sow the ground, and bread of the increase of the earth; It will be fat and plentiful. In that day your cattle will feed in large pastures.

Matthew 6:32-34 AMP

For the [pagan] Gentiles eagerly seek all these things; [but do not worry,] for your heavenly Father knows that you need them. But first and most importantly seek (aim at, strive after) His kingdom and His righteousness [His way of doing and being right—the attitude and character of God], and all these things will be given to you also. So do not worry about tomorrow; for tomorrow will worry about itself. Each day has enough trouble of its own.

Philippians 4:6-7 NIV

Do not be anxious about anything, but in every situation, by prayer and petition, with thanksgiving, present your requests to God. And the peace of God, which transcends all understanding, will guard your hearts and your minds in Christ Jesus.

1 Peter 5:7 NKJV

Casting all your care upon Him, for He cares for you.

Mark 10:45 NKJV

For even the Son of Man did not come to be served, but to serve, and to give His life a ransom for many.

Psalm 85:12 NLT

Yes, the Lord pours down his blessings. Our land will yield its bountiful harvest.

Psalm 23:1 NKJV

The Lord is my shepherd; I shall not want.

2 Corinthians 9:8 NIV

And God is able to bless you abundantly, so that in all things at all times, having all that you need, you will abound in every good work.

Nehemiah 9:15 NKJV

You gave them bread from heaven for their hunger, And brought them water out of the rock for their thirst, And told them to go in to possess the land Which You had sworn to give them.

Psalm 36:8 KJV

They shall be abundantly satisfied with the fatness of thy house; and thou shalt make them drink of the river of thy pleasures.

Psalm 104:24 KJV

O Lord, how manifold are thy works! in wisdom hast thou made them all: the earth is full of thy riches.

Psalm 130:7 BSB

O Israel, put your hope in the LORD, for with the LORD is loving devotion, and with Him is redemption in abundance.

Psalm 67:6 KJV

Then shall the earth yield her increase; and God, even our own God, shall bless us.

Psalm 84:11 NKJV

For the Lord God is a sun and shield; The Lord will give grace and glory; No good thing will He withhold From those who walk uprightly.

Ezekiel 34:27 NKJV

Then the trees of the field shall yield their fruit, and the earth shall yield her increase. They shall be safe in their land; and they shall know that I am the Lord, when I have broken the bands of their yoke and delivered them from the hand of those who enslaved them.

Mark 11:24 AMP

For this reason I am telling you, whatever things you ask for in prayer [in accordance with God's will], believe [with confident trust] that you have received them, and they will be given to you.

2 Corinthians 3:5 NKJV

Not that we are sufficient of ourselves to think of anything as being from ourselves, but our sufficiency is from God.

Philippians 4:13 AMP

I can do all things [which He has called me to do] through Him who strengthens and empowers me [to fulfill His purpose—I am self-sufficient in Christ's sufficiency; I am ready for anything and equal to anything through Him who infuses me with inner strength and confident peace.]

Ephesians 1:3 NKJV

Blessed be the God and Father of our Lord Jesus Christ, who has blessed us with every spiritual blessing in the heavenly places in Christ.

John 15:7-8 ESV

If you abide in me, and my words abide in you, ask whatever you wish, and it will be done for you. By this my Father is glorified, that you bear much fruit and so prove to be my disciples.

John 14:13-14 KJV

And whatsoever ye shall ask in my name, that will I do, that the Father may be glorified in the Son. If ye shall ask any thing in my name, I will do it.

John 16:23-24 BSB

In that day you will no longer ask Me anything. Truly, truly, I tell you, whatever you ask the Father in My name, He will give you. 24Until now you have not asked for anything in My name. Ask and you will receive, so that your joy may be complete.

Psalm 68:5-6 AMP

A father of the fatherless and a judge and protector of the widows, is God in His holy habitation. God makes a home for the lonely; He leads the prisoners into prosperity, only the stubborn and rebellious dwell in a parched land.

Romans 8:32 KJV

He that spared not his own Son, but delivered him up for us all, how shall he not with him also freely give us all things?

Matthew 21:22 ESV

And whatever you ask in prayer, you will receive, if you have faith.

Proverbs 8:20-21 NKJV

I traverse the way of righteousness, in the midst of the paths of justice, that I may cause those who love me to inherit wealth, that I may fill their treasuries.

Isaiah 48:17 ESV

I am the Lord your God, who teaches you to profit, who leads you in the way you should go.

Isaiah 55:10-11 NKJV

For as the rain comes down, and the snow from heaven, and do not return there, but water the earth, and make it bring forth and bud, that it may give seed to the sower and bread to the eater, so shall My word be that goes forth from My mouth; It shall not return to Me void, but it shall accomplish what I please, and it shall prosper in the thing for which I sent it.

3 John 2 KJV

Beloved, I wish above all things that thou mayest prosper and be in health, even as thy soul prospereth.

Luke 11:13 ESV

If you then, who are evil, know how to give good gifts to your children, how much more will the heavenly Father give the Holy Spirit to those who ask him!

John 15:16 AMP

You have not chosen Me, but I have chosen you and I have appointed and placed and purposefully planted you, so that you would go and bear fruit and keep on bearing, and that your fruit will remain and be lasting, so that whatever you ask of the Father in My name [as My representative] He may give to you.

Isaiah 54:1 BSB

Shout for joy, O barren woman, who bears no children; break forth in song and cry aloud, you who have never travailed; because more are the children of the desolate woman than of her who has a husband.

JEHOVAH MEKODDISHKEM

Jehovah Who Sanctifies

Leviticus 22:32 ESV

And you shall not profane my holy name, that I may be sanctified among the people of Israel. I am the Lord who sanctifies you.

1 Peter 2:9-10 BSB

But you are a chosen people, a royal priesthood, a holy nation, a people for God's own possession, to proclaim the virtues of Him who called you out of darkness into His marvelous light. Once you were not a people, but now you are the people of God; once you had not received mercy, but now you have received mercy.

Hebrews 2:11 AMP

Both Jesus who sanctifies and those who are sanctified [that is, spiritually transformed, made holy, and set apart for God's purpose] are all from one Father; for this reason He is not ashamed to call them brothers and sisters,

Hebrews 10:10 AMP

And in accordance with this will [of God] we [who believe in the message of salvation] have been sanctified [that is, set apart as holy for God and His purposes] through the offering of the body of Jesus Christ (the Messiah, the Anointed) once for all.

1 Corinthians 6:11 NKJV

And such were some of you. But you were washed, but you were sanctified, but you were justified in the name of the Lord Jesus and by the Spirit of our God.

Exodus 31:12-13 NKJV

And the Lord spoke to Moses, saying, "Speak also to the children of Israel, saying: 'Surely My Sabbaths you shall keep, for it is a sign between Me and you throughout your generations, that you may know that I am the Lord who sanctifies you.'"

1 Peter 1:15-16 NKJV

But as He who called you is holy, you also be holy in all your conduct, because it is written, "Be holy, for I am holy."

Hebrews 13:12 AMP

Therefore Jesus also suffered and died outside the [city] gate so that He might sanctify and set apart for God as holy the people [who believe] through [the shedding of] His own blood.

1 Thessalonians 5:23-24 AMP

Now may the God of peace Himself sanctify you through and through [that is, separate you from profane and vulgar things, make you pure and whole and undamaged—consecrated to Him—set apart for His purpose]; and may your spirit and soul and body be kept complete and [be found] blameless at the coming of our Lord Jesus Christ. Faithful and absolutely trustworthy is He who is calling you [to Himself for your salvation], and He will do it [He will fulfill His call by making you holy, guarding you, watching over you, and protecting you as His own].

Luke 4:18-19 BSB

The Spirit of the Lord is on Me, because He has anointed Me to preach good news to the poor. He has sent Me to proclaim liberty to the captives and recovery of sight to the blind, to release the oppressed, to proclaim the year of the Lord's favor.

1 John 4:8-10 AMP

The one who does not love has not become acquainted with God [does not and never did know Him], for God is love. [He is the originator of love, and it is an enduring attribute of His nature.] By this the love of God was displayed in us, in that God has sent His [One and] only begotten Son [the One who is truly unique, the only One of His kind] into the world so that we might live through Him. In this is love, not that we loved God, but that He loved us and sent His Son to be the propitiation [that is, the atoning sacrifice, and the satisfying offering] for our sins [fulfilling God's requirement for justice against sin and placating His wrath].

Ephesians 2:4-7 BSB

But because of His great love for us, God, who is rich in mercy, made us alive with Christ even when we were dead in our trespasses. It is by grace you have been saved! And God raised us up with Christ and seated us with Him in the heavenly realms in Christ Jesus, in order that in the coming ages He might display the surpassing riches of His grace, demonstrated by His kindness to us in Christ Jesus.

2 Peter 3:9 ESV

The Lord is not slow to fulfill his promise as some count slowness, but is patient toward you, not wishing that any should perish, but that all should reach repentance.

1 Corinthians 1:18 KJV

For the preaching of the cross is to them that perish foolishness; but unto us which are saved it is the power of God.

1 Timothy 1:14-15 KJV

And the grace of our Lord was exceeding abundant with faith and love which is in Christ Jesus. This is a faithful saying, and worthy of all acceptation, that Christ Jesus came into the world to save sinners; of whom I am chief.

Psalm 32:1-2 KJV

Blessed is he whose transgression is forgiven, whose sin is covered. Blessed is the man unto whom the Lord imputeth not iniquity, and in whose spirit there is no guile.

Acts 3:19-20 AMP

So repent [change your inner self—your old way of thinking, regret past sins] and return [to God—seek His purpose for your life], so that your sins may be wiped away [blotted out, completely erased], so that times of refreshing may come from the presence of the Lord [restoring you like a cool wind on a hot day]; and that He may send [to you] Jesus, the Christ, who has been appointed for you.

Acts 10:43 AMP

All the prophets testify about Him, that through His name everyone who believes in Him [whoever trusts in and relies on Him, accepting Him as Savior and Messiah] receives forgiveness of sins.

Romans 5:1-2 BSB

Therefore, since we have been justified through faith, we have peace with God through our Lord Jesus Christ, through whom we have gained access by faith into this grace in which we stand. And we rejoice in the hope of the glory of God.

Romans 6:4 BSB

We were therefore buried with Him through baptism into death, in order that, just as Christ was raised from the dead through the glory of the Father, we too may walk in newness of life.

Romans 6:6-8 BSB

We know that our old self was crucified with Him so that the body of sin might be rendered powerless, that we should no longer be slaves to sin. For anyone who has died has been freed from sin. Now if we died with Christ, we believe that we will also live with Him.

1 Corinthians 1:2 ESV

To the church of God that is in Corinth, to those sanctified in Christ Jesus, called to be saints together with all those who in every place call upon the name of our Lord Jesus Christ, both their Lord and ours.

2 Corinthians 5:17-19 AMP

Therefore if anyone is in Christ [that is, grafted in, joined to Him by faith in Him as Savior], he is a new creature [reborn and renewed by the Holy Spirit]; the old things [the previous moral and spiritual condition] have passed away. Behold, new things have come [because spiritual awakening brings a new life]. But all these things are from God, who reconciled us to Himself through Christ [making us acceptable to Him] and gave us the ministry of reconciliation [so that by our example we might bring others to Him], that is, that God was in Christ reconciling the world to Himself, not counting people's sins against them [but canceling them]. And He has committed to us the message of reconciliation [that is, restoration to favor with God].

Colossians 1:22 NKJV

In the body of His flesh through death, to present you holy, and blameless, and above reproach in His sight.

2 Thessalonians 2:13 BSB

But we should always thank God for you, brothers who are loved by the Lord, because God has chosen you from the beginning to be saved by the sanctification of the Spirit and by faith in the truth.

Jude 1:24-25 AMP

Now to Him who is able to keep you from stumbling or falling into sin, and to present you unblemished [blameless and faultless] in the presence of His glory with triumphant joy and unspeakable delight, to the only God our Savior, through Jesus Christ our Lord, be glory, majesty, dominion, and power, before all time and now and forever. Amen.

JEHOVAH NISSI

The Lord Is My Banner

Exodus 17:15-16 NLT

*Moses built an altar there and named it Yahweh-
Nissi (which means "the Lord is my banner").
He said, "They have raised their fist against the
Lord's throne, so now the Lord will be at war
with Amalek generation after generation."*

John 12:32 ESV

And I, when I am lifted up from the earth, will draw all people to myself.

Isaiah 11:10 NLT

In that day the heir to David's throne will be a banner of salvation to all the world. The nations will rally to him, and the land where he lives will be a glorious place.

John 3:14-15 BSB

Just as Moses lifted up the snake in the wilderness, so the Son of Man must be lifted up, that everyone who believes in Him may have eternal life.

Psalm 60:4 AMP

You have set up a banner for those who fear You [with awe-inspired reverence and submissive wonder—a banner to shield them from attack], a banner that may be displayed because of the truth. Selah.

Song of Solomon 2:4 ESV

He brought me to the banqueting house, and his banner over me was love.

Psalm 55:18 NKJV

He has redeemed my soul in peace from the battle that was against me, For there were many against me.

2 Samuel 22:17-20 BSB

He reached down from on high and took hold of me; He drew me out of deep waters. He rescued me from my powerful enemy, from foes too mighty for me. They confronted me in my day of calamity, but the LORD was my support. He brought me out into the open; He rescued me because He delighted in me.

Isaiah 62:10 BSB

Go out, go out through the gates; prepare the way for the people! Build it up, build up the highway; clear away the stones; raise a banner for the nations!

Deuteronomy 20:3-4 KJV

And shall say unto them, Hear, O Israel, ye approach this day unto battle against your enemies: let not your hearts faint, fear not, and do not tremble, neither be ye terrified because of them; For the Lord your God is he that goeth with you, to fight for you against your enemies, to save you.

Ephesians 6:10-12 ESV

Finally, be strong in the Lord and in the strength of his might. Put on the whole armor of God, that you may be able to stand against the schemes of the devil. For we do not wrestle against flesh and blood, but against the rulers, against the authorities, against the cosmic powers over this present darkness, against the spiritual forces of evil in the heavenly places.

Psalm 48:3 NIV

God is in her citadels; he has shown himself to be her fortress.

Jeremiah 15:20 NLT

They will fight against you like an attacking army, but I will make you as secure as a fortified wall of bronze. They will not conquer you, for I am with you to protect and rescue you. I, the Lord, have spoken!

Jeremiah 42:11-12 AMP

"Do not be afraid of the king of Babylon, whom you now fear [as if he were deity]; do not be afraid of him," says the Lord, "for [he is a mere man, but I am the living, omniscient God and] I am with you [always] to protect you and to deliver you from his hand. And I will show you compassion, so that he will have compassion on you and restore you to your own land."

Psalm 9:9 KJV

The Lord also will be a refuge for the oppressed, a refuge in times of trouble.

John 8:28 NKJV

Then Jesus said to them, "When you lift up the Son of Man, then you will know that I am He, and that I do nothing of Myself; but as My Father taught Me, I speak these things."

Isaiah 59:19 NKJV

So shall they fear The name of the Lord from the west, and His glory from the rising of the sun; When the enemy comes in like a flood, the Spirit of the Lord will lift up a standard against him.

Psalm 91:1, 4 AMP

He who dwells in the shelter of the Most High Will remain secure and rest in the shadow of the Almighty [whose power no enemy can withstand]. ...He will cover you and completely protect you with His pinions, And under His wings you will find refuge; His faithfulness is a shield and a wall.

Psalm 3:6 NKJV

I will not be afraid of ten thousands of people Who have set themselves against me all around.

Psalm 27:1-3 ESV

The Lord is my light and my salvation; whom shall I fear? The Lord is the stronghold of my life; of whom shall I be afraid? When evildoers assail me to eat up my flesh, my adversaries and foes, it is they who stumble and fall. Though an army encamp against me, my heart shall not fear; though war arise against me, yet I will be confident.

2 Kings 6:16 NKJV

So he answered, "Do not fear, for those who are with us are more than those who are with them."

2 Chronicles 32:7-8 NIV

"Be strong and courageous. Do not be afraid or discouraged because of the king of Assyria and the vast army with him, for there is a greater power with us than with him. With him is only the arm of flesh, but with us is the Lord our God to help us and to fight our battles." And the people gained confidence from what Hezekiah the king of Judah said.

Isaiah 41:10 NKJV

Fear not, for I am with you; Be not dismayed, for I am your God. I will strengthen you, Yes, I will help you, I will uphold you with My righteous right hand.

Jeremiah 1:19 KJV

And they shall fight against thee; but they shall not prevail against thee; for I am with thee, saith the Lord, to deliver thee.

Deuteronomy 31:6 NKJV

Be strong and of good courage, do not fear nor be afraid of them; for the Lord your God, He is the One who goes with you. He will not leave you nor forsake you.

Deuteronomy 3:22 NIV

Do not be afraid of them; the Lord your God himself will fight for you.

JEHOVAH RAPHA

The Lord Our Healer
Jehovah Heals

Exodus 15:26 NLT

*He said, "If you will listen carefully to the voice of
the Lord your God and do what is right in his sight,
obeying his commands and keeping all his decrees, then
I will not make you suffer any of the diseases I sent
on the Egyptians; for I am the Lord who heals you."*

1 Peter 2:4 NKJV

Coming to Him as to a living stone, rejected indeed by men, but chosen by God and precious.

Psalm 103:2-5 NKJV

Bless the Lord, O my soul, and forget not all His benefits: Who forgives all your iniquities, Who heals all your diseases, Who redeems your life from destruction, Who crowns you with lovingkindness and tender mercies, Who satisfies your mouth with good things, So that your youth is renewed like the eagle's.

Psalm 147:3 ESV

He heals the brokenhearted and binds up their wounds.

Matthew 12:15 NKJV

But when Jesus knew it, He withdrew from there. And great multitudes followed Him, and He healed them all.

Isaiah 53:3-5 AMP

He was despised and rejected by men, a Man of sorrows and pain and acquainted with grief; And like One from whom men hide their faces He was despised, and we did not appreciate His worth or esteem Him. But [in fact] He has borne our griefs, and He has carried our sorrows and pains; Yet we [ignorantly] assumed that He was stricken, struck down by God and degraded and humiliated [by Him]. But He was wounded for our transgressions, He was crushed for our wickedness [our sin, our injustice, our wrongdoing]; The punishment [required] for our well-being fell on Him, and by His stripes (wounds) we are healed.

James 5:13-16 BSB

Is any one of you suffering? He should pray. Is anyone cheerful? He should sing praises. Is any one of you sick? He should call the elders of the church to pray over him and anoint him with oil in the name of the Lord. And the prayer offered in faith will restore the one who is sick. The Lord will raise him up. If he has sinned, he will be forgiven. Therefore confess your sins to each other and pray for each other so that you may be healed. The prayer of a righteous man has great power to prevail.

Jeremiah 33:6-8 NIV

Nevertheless, I will bring health and healing to it; I will heal my people and will let them enjoy abundant peace and security. I will bring Judah and Israel back from captivity and will rebuild them as they were before. I will cleanse them from all the sin they have committed against me and will forgive all their sins of rebellion against me.

Luke 5:12-13 NKJV

And it happened when He was in a certain city, that behold, a man who was full of leprosy saw Jesus; and he fell on his face and implored Him, saying, "Lord, if You are willing, You can make me clean." Then He put out His hand and touched him, saying, "I am willing; be cleansed." Immediately the leprosy left him.

Malachi 4:2-3 BSB

"But for you who fear My name, the sun of righteousness will rise with healing in its wings, and you will go out and leap like calves from the stall. Then you will trample the wicked, for they will be ashes under the soles of your feet on the day I am preparing," says the LORD of Hosts.

Exodus 23:25 NKJV

So you shall serve the Lord your God, and He will bless your bread and your water. And I will take sickness away from the midst of you.

Isaiah 53:11 NASB 1995

As a result of the anguish of His soul, He will see it and be satisfied; By His knowledge the Righteous One, My Servant, will justify the many, as He will bear their iniquities.

Psalm 30:2 ESV

O Lord my God, I cried to you for help, and you have healed me.

Psalm 6:2 BSB

Be merciful to me, O LORD, for I am frail; heal me, O LORD, for my bones are in agony.

Psalm 107:19-20 KJV

Then they cry unto the Lord in their trouble, and he saveth them out of their distresses. He sent his word, and healed them, and delivered them from their destructions.

Matthew 8:8-9 BSB

The centurion answered, "Lord, I am not worthy to have You come under my roof. But just say the word, and my servant will be healed. For I myself am a man under authority, with soldiers under me. I tell one to go, and he goes; and another to come, and he comes. I tell my servant to do something, and he does it."

Job 33:28 ESV

He has redeemed my soul from going down into the pit, and my life shall look upon the light.

Psalm 56:13 NLT

For you have rescued me from death; you have kept my feet from slipping. So now I can walk in your presence, O God, in your life-giving light.

Psalm 41:4 KJV

I said, Lord, be merciful unto me: heal my soul; for I have sinned against thee.

Matthew 4:23 NIV

Jesus went throughout Galilee, teaching in their synagogues, proclaiming the good news of the kingdom, and healing every disease and sickness among the people.

Luke 9:11 NKJV

But when the multitudes knew it, they followed Him; and He received them and spoke to them about the kingdom of God, and healed those who had need of healing.

Matthew 4:24 ESV

So his fame spread throughout all Syria, and they brought him all the sick, those afflicted with various diseases and pains, those oppressed by demons, those having seizures, and paralytics, and he healed them.

Matthew 8:7-8 NIV

Jesus said to him, "Shall I come and heal him?" The centurion replied, "Lord, I do not deserve to have you come under my roof. But just say the word, and my servant will be healed."

2 Kings 5:14 NKJV

So he went down and dipped seven times in the Jordan, according to the saying of the man of God; and his flesh was restored like the flesh of a little child, and he was clean.

John 4:50-53 BSB

"Go," said Jesus. "Your son will live." The man took Jesus at His word and departed. And while he was still on the way, his servants met him with the news that his boy was alive. So he inquired as to the hour when his son had recovered, and they told him, "The fever left him yesterday at the seventh hour." Then the father realized that this was the very hour in which Jesus had told him, "Your son will live." And he and all his household believed.

Luke 4:39 BSB

And He stood over her and rebuked the fever, and it left her. And she got up at once and began to serve them.

Isaiah 58:8 AMP

Then your light will break out like the dawn, and your healing (restoration, new life) will quickly spring forth; Your righteousness will go before you [leading you to peace and prosperity], the glory of the Lord will be your rear guard.

Jeremiah 3:22 NLT

"My wayward children," says the Lord, "come back to me, and I will heal your wayward hearts." "Yes, we're coming," the people reply, "for you are the Lord our God."

Jeremiah 17:14 NKJV

Heal me, O Lord, and I shall be healed; Save me, and I shall be saved, for You are my praise.

Mark 16:15-18 KJV

And he said unto them, Go ye into all the world, and preach the gospel to every creature. He that believeth and is baptized shall be saved; but he that believeth not shall be damned. And these signs shall follow them that believe; In my name shall they cast out devils; they shall speak with new tongues; They shall take up serpents; and if they drink any deadly thing, it shall not hurt them; they shall lay hands on the sick, and they shall recover.

JEHOVAH ROHI

The Lord Is My Shepherd

Psalm 23:1 NKJV
The Lord is my shepherd; I shall not want.

Psalm 23:1-6 NKJV

The Lord is my shepherd; I shall not want. He makes me to lie down in green pastures; He leads me beside the still waters. He restores my soul; He leads me in the paths of righteousness for His name's sake. Yea, though I walk through the valley of the shadow of death, I will fear no evil; For You are with me; Your rod and Your staff, they comfort me. You prepare a table before me in the presence of my enemies; You anoint my head with oil; My cup runs over. Surely goodness and mercy shall follow me all the days of my life; And I will dwell in the house of the Lord forever.

Isaiah 53:6-7 ESV

All we like sheep have gone astray; we have turned—every one—to his own way; and the Lord has laid on him the iniquity of us all. He was oppressed, and he was afflicted, yet he opened not his mouth; like a lamb that is led to the slaughter, and like a sheep that before its shearers is silent, so he opened not his mouth.

John 10:11-18 KJV

I am the good shepherd: the good shepherd giveth his life for the sheep. But he that is an hireling, and not the shepherd, whose own the sheep are not, seeth the wolf coming, and leaveth the sheep, and fleeth: and the wolf catcheth them, and scattereth the sheep. The hireling fleeth, because he is an hireling, and careth not for the sheep. I am the good shepherd, and know my sheep, and am known of mine. As the Father knoweth me, even so know I the Father: and I lay down my life for the sheep. And other sheep I have, which are not of this fold: them also I must bring, and they shall hear my voice; and there shall be one fold, and one shepherd. Therefore doth my Father love me, because I lay down my life, that I might take it again. No man taketh it from me, but I lay it down of myself. I have power to lay it down, and I have power to take it again. This commandment have I received of my Father.

Hebrews 13:20-21 ESV

Now may the God of peace who brought again from the dead our Lord Jesus, the great shepherd of the sheep, by the blood of the eternal covenant, equip you with everything good that you may do his will, working in us that which is pleasing in his sight, through Jesus Christ, to whom be glory forever and ever. Amen.

Revelation 7:17 NLT

For the Lamb on the throne will be their Shepherd. He will lead them to springs of life-giving water. And God will wipe every tear from their eyes.

1 Peter 2:25 AMP

For you were continually wandering like [so many] sheep, but now you have come back to the Shepherd and Guardian of your souls.

Proverbs 3:6 NKJV

In all your ways acknowledge Him, and He shall direct your paths.

Jeremiah 24:6-7 NLT

I will watch over and care for them, and I will bring them back here again. I will build them up and not tear them down. I will plant them and not uproot them. I will give them hearts that recognize me as the Lord. They will be my people, and I will be their God, for they will return to me wholeheartedly.

Jeremiah 29:11-13 NKJV

For I know the thoughts that I think toward you, says the Lord, thoughts of peace and not of evil, to give you a future and a hope. Then you will call upon Me and go and pray to Me, and I will listen to you. And you will seek Me and find Me, when you search for Me with all your heart.

Psalm 119:176 ESV

I have gone astray like a lost sheep; seek your servant, for I do not forget your commandments.

1 Peter 5:4 NKJV

And when the Chief Shepherd appears, you will receive the crown of glory that does not fade away.

Proverbs 16:9 BSB

A man's heart plans his course, but the LORD determines his steps.

Psalm 32:8 ESV

I will instruct you and teach you in the way you should go; I will counsel you with my eye upon you.

Psalm 37:23 AMP

The steps of a [good and righteous] man are directed and established by the Lord, and He delights in his way [and blesses his path].

Jeremiah 10:23 AMP

O Lord, I know that the path of [life of] a man is not in himself; It is not within [the limited ability of] man [even one at his best] to choose and direct his steps [in life].

Isaiah 26:7 BSB

The path of the righteous is level; You clear a straight path for the upright.

Psalm 25:4-5 BSB

Show me Your ways, O LORD; teach me Your paths. Guide me in Your truth and teach me, for You are the God of my salvation; all day long I wait for You.

Isaiah 42:16 AMP

I will lead the blind by a way they do not know; I will guide them in paths that they do not know. I will make darkness into light before them And rugged places into plains. These things I will do [for them], And I will not leave them abandoned or undone.

Isaiah 52:12 ESV

For you shall not go out in haste, and you shall not go in flight, for the Lord will go before you, and the God of Israel will be your rear guard.

Luke 3:5 KJV

Every valley shall be filled, and every mountain and hill shall be brought low; and the crooked shall be made straight, and the rough ways shall be made smooth.

Isaiah 30:21 NLT

Your own ears will hear him. Right behind you a voice will say, "This is the way you should go," whether to the right or to the left.

Isaiah 40:4 NKJV

Every valley shall be exalted and every mountain and hill brought low; The crooked places shall be made]straight and the rough places smooth.

Isaiah 45:2 KJV

I will go before thee, and make the crooked places straight: I will break in pieces the gates of brass, and cut in sunder the bars of iron.

Psalm 43:3 NIV

Send me your light and your faithful care, let them lead me; let them bring me to your holy mountain, to the place where you dwell.

Isaiah 48:15 NKJV

I, even I, have spoken; Yes, I have called him, I have brought him, and his way will prosper.

JEHOVAH SHALOM

The Lord Our Peace
Jehovah Is Peace

Judges 6:22-24 BSB

When Gideon realized that it was the angel of the LORD, he said, "Oh no, Lord GOD! I have seen the angel of the LORD face to face!" But the LORD said to him, "Peace be with you. Do not be afraid, for you will not die." So Gideon built an altar to the LORD there and called it The LORD Is Peace. To this day it stands in Ophrah of the Abiezrites.

1 Peter 5:7 AMP

Casting all your cares [all your anxieties, all your worries, and all your concerns, once and for all] on Him, for He cares about you [with deepest affection, and watches over you very carefully].

Philippians 4:6-7 ESV

Do not be anxious about anything, but in everything by prayer and supplication with thanksgiving let your requests be made known to God. 7 And the peace of God, which surpasses all understanding, will guard your hearts and your minds in Christ Jesus.

Matthew 6:33-34 NKJV

But seek first the kingdom of God and His righteousness, and all these things shall be added to you. Therefore do not worry about tomorrow, for tomorrow will worry about its own things. Sufficient for the day is its own trouble.

2 Thessalonians 2:16-17 KJV

Now our Lord Jesus Christ himself, and God, even our Father, which hath loved us, and hath given us everlasting consolation and good hope through grace, Comfort your hearts, and stablish you in every good word and work.

Isaiah 9:6 NKJV

For unto us a Child is born, unto us a Son is given; And the government will be upon His shoulder. And His name will be called Wonderful, Counselor, Mighty God, Everlasting Father, Prince of Peace.

John 14:27 ESV

Peace I leave with you; my peace I give to you. Not as the world gives do I give to you. Let not your hearts be troubled, neither let them be afraid.

Romans 14:17 KJV

For the kingdom of God is not meat and drink; but righteousness, and peace, and joy in the Holy Ghost.

Jeremiah 33:6 KJV

Behold, I will bring it health and cure, and I will cure them, and will reveal unto them the abundance of peace and truth.

2 Thessalonians 3:16 AMP

Now may the Lord of peace Himself grant you His peace at all times and in every way [that peace and spiritual well-being that comes to those who walk with Him, regardless of life's circumstances]. The Lord be with you all.

Luke 2:14 ESV

Glory to God in the highest, and on earth peace among those with whom he is pleased!

Romans 5:1-2 NLT

Therefore, since we have been made right in God's sight by faith, we have peace with God because of what Jesus Christ our Lord has done for us. Because of our faith, Christ has brought us into this place of undeserved privilege where we now stand, and we confidently and joyfully look forward to sharing God's glory.

Ephesians 2:14-19 ESV

For he himself is our peace, who has made us both one and has broken down in his flesh the dividing wall of hostility by abolishing the law of commandments expressed in ordinances, that he might create in himself one new man in place of the two, so making peace, and might reconcile us both to God in one body through the cross, thereby killing the hostility. And he came and preached peace to you who were far off and peace to those who were near. For through him we both have access in one Spirit to the Father. So then you are no longer strangers and aliens, but you are fellow citizens with the saints and members of the household of God.

Colossians 1:19-20 NKJV

For it pleased the Father that in Him all the fullness should dwell, and by Him to reconcile all things to Himself, by Him, whether things on earth or things in heaven, having made peace through the blood of His cross.

Numbers 6:24-27 NKJV

"The Lord bless you and keep you; The Lord make His face shine upon you, and be gracious to you; The Lord lift up His countenance upon you, and give you peace." So they shall put My name on the children of Israel, and I will bless them.

John 20:21-22 BSB

Again Jesus said to them, "Peace be with you. As the Father has sent Me, so also I am sending you." When He had said this, He breathed on them and said, "Receive the Holy Spirit."

Luke 12:11 ESV

And when they bring you before the synagogues and the rulers and the authorities, do not be anxious about how you should defend yourself or what you should say.

Deuteronomy 1:21 NKJV

Look, the Lord your God has set the land before you; go up and possess it, as the Lord God of your fathers has spoken to you; do not fear or be discouraged.

Isaiah 54:10, 13-14 BSB

"Though the mountains may be removed and the hills may be shaken, My loving devotion will not depart from you, and My covenant of peace will not be broken," says the LORD, who has compassion on you. ...Then all your sons will be taught by the LORD, and great will be their prosperity. In righteousness you will be established, far from oppression, for you will have no fear. Terror will be far removed, for it will not come near you.

Isaiah 66:12 ESV

For thus says the Lord: "Behold, I will extend peace to her like a river, and the glory of the nations like an overflowing stream; and you shall nurse, you shall be carried upon her hip, and bounced upon her knees."

John 16:33 AMP

I have told you these things, so that in Me you may have [perfect] peace. In the world you have tribulation and distress and suffering, but be courageous [be confident, be undaunted, be filled with joy]; I have overcome the world." [My conquest is accomplished, My victory abiding.]

Colossians 3:15 ESV

And let the peace of Christ rule in your hearts, to which indeed you were called in one body. And be thankful.

Isaiah 55:12 AMP

For you will go out [from exile] with joy and be led forth [by the Lord Himself] with peace; The mountains and the hills will break forth into shouts of joy before you, and all the trees of the field will clap their hands.

Jeremiah 29:11 ESV

For I know the plans I have for you, declares the Lord, plans for welfare and not for evil, to give you a future and a hope.

Psalm 34:14 KJV

Depart from evil, and do good; seek peace, and pursue it.

Psalm 4:8 BSB

I will lie down and sleep in peace, for You alone, O LORD, make me dwell in safety.

Psalm 85:8 NLT

I listen carefully to what God the Lord is saying, for he speaks peace to his faithful people. But let them not return to their foolish ways.

Psalm 119:165 BSB

Abundant peace belongs to those who love Your instruction; nothing can make them stumble.

Isaiah 26:3 KJV

Thou wilt keep him in perfect peace, whose mind is stayed on thee: because he trusteth in thee.

Luke 1:76-79 NKJV

And you, child, will be called the prophet of the Highest; For you will go before the face of the Lord to prepare His ways, to give knowledge of salvation to His people by the remission of their sins, through the tender mercy of our God, with which the Dayspring from on high has visited us; To give light to those who sit in darkness and the shadow of death, to guide our feet into the way of peace.

John 14:27 AMP

Peace I leave with you; My [perfect] peace I give to you; not as the world gives do I give to you. Do not let your heart be troubled, nor let it be afraid. [Let My perfect peace calm you in every circumstance and give you courage and strength for every challenge.]

Romans 1:7 NIV

To all in Rome who are loved by God and called to be his holy people: Grace and peace to you from God our Father and from the Lord Jesus Christ.

2 Timothy 2:22 NLT

Run from anything that stimulates youthful lusts. Instead, pursue righteous living, faithfulness, love, and peace. Enjoy the companionship of those who call on the Lord with pure hearts.

2 Peter 1:2 BSB

Grace and peace be multiplied to you through the knowledge of God and of Jesus our Lord.

Luke 1:79 KJV

To give light to them that sit in darkness and in the shadow of death, to guide our feet into the way of peace.

Psalm 94:18-19 AMP

If I say, "My foot has slipped," Your compassion and lovingkindness, O Lord, will hold me up. When my anxious thoughts multiply within me, Your comforts delight me.

Daniel 10:19 AMP

He said, "O man, highly regarded and greatly beloved, do not be afraid. Peace be to you; take courage and be strong." Now when he had spoken to me, I was strengthened and said, "Let my lord speak, for you have strengthened me."

JEHOVAH SHAMMAH

The Lord Is Present
Jehovah Is There

Ezekiel 48:35 NKJV

All the way around shall be eighteen thousand cubits; and the name of the city from that day shall be: THE LORD IS THERE.

John 14:15-18 NKJV

If you love Me, keep My commandments. And I will pray the Father, and He will give you another Helper, that He may abide with you forever— the Spirit of truth, whom the world cannot receive, because it neither sees Him nor knows Him; but you know Him, for He dwells with you and will be in you. I will not leave you orphans; I will come to you.

Matthew 18:19-20 KJV

Again I say unto you, That if two of you shall agree on earth as touching any thing that they shall ask, it shall be done for them of my Father which is in heaven. For where two or three are gathered together in my name, there am I in the midst of them.

Deuteronomy 30:19-20 KJV

I call heaven and earth to record this day against you, that I have set before you life and death, blessing and cursing: therefore choose life, that both thou and thy seed may live: That thou mayest love the Lord thy God, and that thou mayest obey his voice, and that thou mayest cleave unto him: for he is thy life, and the length of thy days: that thou mayest dwell in the land which the Lord sware unto thy fathers, to Abraham, to Isaac, and to Jacob, to give them.

Jeremiah 24:6-7 BSB

I will keep My eyes on them for good and will return them to this land. I will build them up and not tear them down; I will plant them and not uproot them. I will give them a heart to know Me, that I am the LORD. They will be My people, and I will be their God, for they will return to Me with all their heart.

1 Corinthians 1:9 AMP

God is faithful [He is reliable, trustworthy and ever true to His promise—He can be depended on], and through Him you were called into fellowship with His Son, Jesus Christ our Lord.

1 John 4:16-17 ESV

So we have come to know and to believe the love that God has for us. God is love, and whoever abides in love abides in God, and God abides in him. By this is love perfected with us, so that we may have confidence for the day of judgment, because as he is so also are we in this world.

1 John 4:8 KJV

He that loveth not knoweth not God; for God is love.

1 John 4:12 NLT

No one has ever seen God. But if we love each other, God lives in us, and his love is brought to full expression in us.

Revelation 21:7 KJV

He that overcometh shall inherit all things; and I will be his God, and he shall be my son.

1 Corinthians 3:16 NIV

Don't you know that you yourselves are God's temple and that God's Spirit dwells in your midst?

1 Corinthians 6:19-20 NLT

Don't you realize that your body is the temple of the Holy Spirit, who lives in you and was given to you by God? You do not belong to yourself, for God bought you with a high price. So you must honor God with your body.

Galatians 4:6 AMP

And because you [really] are [His] sons, God has sent the Spirit of His Son into our hearts, crying out,]"Abba! Father!"

Colossians 1:27 AMP

God [in His eternal plan] chose to make known to them how great for the Gentiles are the riches of the glory of this mystery, which is Christ in and among you, the hope and guarantee of [realizing the] glory.

1 John 3:23-24 ESV

And this is his commandment, that we believe in the name of his Son Jesus Christ and love one another, just as he has commanded us. Whoever keeps his commandments abides in God, and God in him. And by this we know that he abides in us, by the Spirit whom he has given us.

Jeremiah 33:3 AMP

Call to Me and I will answer you, and tell you [and even show you] great and mighty things, [things which have been confined and hidden], which you do not know and understand and cannot distinguish.

Isaiah 42:9 AMP

Indeed, the former things have come to pass, Now I declare new things; Before they spring forth I proclaim them to you.

Isaiah 48:6 AMP

You have heard [these things foretold]; look at all this [that has been fulfilled]. And you, will you not declare it? I proclaim to you [specific] new things from this time, Even hidden things which you have not known.

Isaiah 43:19 AMP

Listen carefully, I am about to do a new thing, now it will spring forth; Will you not be aware of it? I will even put a road in the wilderness, rivers in the desert.

Deuteronomy 4:31 NKJV

(For the Lord your God is a merciful God), He will not forsake you nor destroy you, nor forget the covenant of your fathers which He swore to them.

John 15:7 NKJV

If you abide in Me, and My words abide in you, you will ask what you desire, and it shall be done for you.

Revelation 21:3 ESV

And I heard a loud voice from the throne saying, "Behold, the dwelling place of God is with man. He will dwell with them, and they will be his people, and God himself will be with them as their God."

Romans 8:10-12 BSB

But if Christ is in you, your body is dead because of sin, yet your spirit is alive because of righteousness. And if the Spirit of Him who raised Jesus from the dead is living in you, He who raised Christ Jesus from the dead will also give life to your mortal bodies through His Spirit, who lives in you. Therefore, brothers, we have an obligation, but it is not to the flesh, to live according to it.

Matthew 28:20 AMP

Teaching them to observe everything that I have commanded you; and lo, I am with you always [remaining with you perpetually—regardless of circumstance, and on every occasion], even to the end of the age.

Zechariah 2:5 KJV

For I, saith the Lord, will be unto her a wall of fire round about, and will be the glory in the midst of her.

Psalm 46:5 ESV

God is in the midst of her; she shall not be moved; God will help her when morning dawns.

Psalm 85:9-10 ESV

Surely his salvation is near to those who fear him, that glory may dwell in our land. Steadfast love and faithfulness meet; righteousness and peace kiss each other.

Psalm 125:2 NKJV

As the mountains surround Jerusalem, so the Lord surrounds His people From this time forth and forever.

Psalm 46:7-11 NKJV

The Lord of hosts is with us; The God of Jacob is our refuge. Selah Come, behold the works of the Lord, who has made desolations in the earth. He makes wars cease to the end of the earth; He breaks the bow and cuts the spear in two; He burns the chariot in the fire. Be still, and know that I am God; I will be exalted among the nations, I will be exalted in the earth! The Lord of hosts is with us; The God of Jacob is our refuge. Selah

Psalm 48:3 KJV

God is known in her palaces for a refuge.

John 1:14 AMP

And the Word (Christ) became flesh, and lived among us; and we [actually] saw His glory, glory as belongs to the [One and] only begotten Son of the Father, [the Son who is truly unique, the only One of His kind, who is] full of grace and truth (absolutely free of deception).

Deuteronomy 4:7 ESV

For what great nation is there that has a god so near to it as the Lord our God is to us, whenever we call upon him?

Psalm 34:18 NLT

The Lord is close to the brokenhearted; he rescues those whose spirits are crushed.

Jeremiah 15:20 AMP

"And I will make you to this people a fortified wall of bronze; They will fight against you, but they will not prevail over you, for I am with you [always] to save you and protect you," says the Lord.

Numbers 14:9 NKJV

Only do not rebel against the Lord, nor fear the people of the land, for they are our bread; their protection has departed from them, and the Lord is with us. Do not fear them.

Galatians 2:20 KJV

I am crucified with Christ: nevertheless I live; yet not I, but Christ liveth in me: and the life which I now live in the flesh I live by the faith of the Son of God, who loved me, and gave himself for me.

Ephesians 3:17 AMP

So that Christ may dwell in your hearts through your faith. And may you, having been [deeply] rooted and [securely] grounded in love.

Colossians 1:27 AMP

God [in His eternal plan] chose to make known to them how great for the Gentiles are the riches of the glory of this mystery, which is Christ in and among you, the hope and guarantee of [realizing the] glory.

John 14:20, 23 NKJV

At that day you will know that I am in My Father, and you in Me, and I in you. …Jesus answered and said to him, "If anyone loves Me, he will keep My word; and My Father will love him, and We will come to him and make Our home with him."

John 15:5 NKJV

I am the vine, you are the branches. He who abides in Me, and I in him, bears much fruit; for without Me you can do nothing.

John 17:22 KJV

And the glory which thou gavest me I have given them; that they may be one, even as we are one.

JEHOVAH TSIDKENU

The Lord Our Righteousness
Jehovah Our Righteousness

Jeremiah 23:5-6 BSB

Behold, the days are coming, declares the LORD, when I will raise up for David a righteous Branch, and He will reign wisely as King and will administer justice and righteousness in the land. In His days Judah will be saved, and Israel will dwell securely. And this is His name by which He will be called: The LORD Our Righteousness.

1 Corinthians 1:30 AMP

But it is from Him that you are in Christ Jesus, who became to us wisdom from God [revealing His plan of salvation], and righteousness [making us acceptable to God], and sanctification [making us holy and setting us apart for God], and redemption [providing our ransom from the penalty for sin].

2 Corinthians 5:21 BSB

God made Him who knew no sin to be sin on our behalf, so that in Him we might become the righteousness of God.

Jeremiah 33:16 ESV

In those days Judah will be saved, and Jerusalem will dwell securely. And this is the name by which it will be called: "The Lord is our righteousness."

Psalm 4:1 ESV

Answer me when I call, O God of my righteousness! You have given me relief when I was in distress. Be gracious to me and hear my prayer!

Romans 4:25 KJV

Who was delivered for our offences, and was raised again for our justification.

Isaiah 53:11 KJV

He shall see of the travail of his soul, and shall be satisfied: by his knowledge shall my righteous servant justify many; for he shall bear their iniquities.

Romans 3:22-26 BSB

And this righteousness from God comes through faith in Jesus Christ to all who believe. There is no distinction, for all have sinned and fall short of the glory of God, and are justified freely by His grace through the redemption that is in Christ Jesus. God presented Him as the atoning sacrifice through faith in His blood, in order to demonstrate His righteousness, because in His forbearance He had passed over the sins committed beforehand. He did this to demonstrate His righteousness at the present time, so as to be just and to justify the one who has faith in Jesus.

2 Corinthians 5:17 NKJV

Therefore, if anyone is in Christ, he is a new creation; old things have passed away; behold, all things have become new.

Philippians 3:7-10 AMP

But whatever former things were gains to me [as I thought then], these things [once regarded as advancements in merit] I have come to consider as loss [absolutely worthless] for the sake of Christ [and the purpose which He has given my life]. But more than that, I count everything as loss compared to the priceless privilege and supreme advantage of knowing Christ Jesus my Lord [and of growing more deeply and thoroughly acquainted with Him—a joy unequaled]. For His sake I have lost everything, and I consider it all garbage, so that I may gain Christ, and may be found in Him [believing and relying on Him], not having any righteousness of my own derived from [my obedience to] the Law and its rituals, but [possessing] that [genuine righteousness] which comes through faith in Christ, the righteousness which comes from God on the basis of faith. And this, so that I may know Him [experientially, becoming more thoroughly acquainted with Him, understanding the remarkable wonders of His Person more completely] and [in that same way experience] the power of His resurrection [which overflows and is active in believers], and [that I may share] the fellowship of His sufferings, by being continually conformed [inwardly into His likeness even] to His death [dying as He did].

Psalm 119:142 AMP

Your righteousness is an everlasting righteousness, and Your law is truth.

Isaiah 42:21 NKJV

The Lord is well pleased for His righteousness' sake; He will exalt the law and make it honorable.

Ezekial 36:25-28 NIV

I will sprinkle clean water on you, and you will be clean; I will cleanse you from all your impurities and from all your idols. I will give you a new heart and put a new spirit in you; I will remove from you your heart of stone and give you a heart of flesh. And I will put my Spirit in you and move you to follow my decrees and be careful to keep my laws. Then you will live in the land I gave your ancestors; you will be my people, and I will be your God.

1 John 1:9 NIV

If we confess our sins, he is faithful and just and will forgive us our sins and purify us from all unrighteousness.

1 Peter 2:24 ESV

He himself bore our sins in his body on the tree, that we might die to sin and live to righteousness. By his wounds you have been healed.

Psalm 119:41-42 ESV

Let your steadfast love come to me, O Lord, your salvation according to your promise; then shall I have an answer for him who taunts me, for I trust in your word.

Isaiah 54:17 NKJV

"No weapon formed against you shall prosper, and every tongue which rises against you in judgment you shall condemn. This is the heritage of the servants of the Lord, and their righteousness is from Me," says the Lord.

Psalm 7:17 BSB

I will thank the LORD for His righteousness and sing praise to the name of the LORD Most High.

Psalm 30:11-12 KJV

Thou hast turned for me my mourning into dancing: thou hast put off my sackcloth, and girded me with gladness; To the end that my glory may sing praise to thee, and not be silent. O Lord my God, I will give thanks unto thee for ever.

Romans 5:17 ESV

For if, because of one man's trespass, death reigned through that one man, much more will those who receive the abundance of grace and the free gift of righteousness reign in life through the one man Jesus Christ.

Romans 5:20-21 AMP

But the Law came to increase and expand [the awareness of] the trespass [by defining and unmasking sin]. But where sin increased, [God's remarkable, gracious gift of] grace [His unmerited favor] has surpassed it and increased all the more, so that, as sin reigned in death, so also grace would reign through righteousness which brings eternal life through Jesus Christ our Lord.

Romans 8:9-12 NIV

You, however, are not in the realm of the flesh but are in the realm of the Spirit, if indeed the Spirit of God lives in you. And if anyone does not have the Spirit of Christ, they do not belong to Christ. But if Christ is in you, then even though your body is subject to death because of sin, the Spirit gives life because of righteousness. And if the Spirit of him who raised Jesus from the dead is living in you, he who raised Christ from the dead will also give life to your mortal bodies because of his Spirit who lives in you. Therefore, brothers and sisters, we have an obligation—but it is not to the flesh, to live according to it.

Romans 10:4 BSB

For Christ is the end of the law, to bring righteousness to everyone who believes.

Galatians 5:5 NKJV

For we through the Spirit eagerly wait for the hope of righteousness by faith.

Ephesians 4:22-24 NIV

You were taught, with regard to your former way of life, to put off your old self, which is being corrupted by its deceitful desires; to be made new in the attitude of your minds; and to put on the new self, created to be like God in true righteousness and holiness.

SAVIOR/REDEEMER

Galatians 3:13-14 ESV

Christ redeemed us from the curse of the law by becoming a curse for us—for it is written, "Cursed is everyone who is hanged on a tree"—so that in Christ Jesus the blessing of Abraham might come to the Gentiles, so that we might receive the promised Spirit through faith.

Ephesians 1:7-10 AMP

In Him we have redemption [that is, our deliverance and salvation] through His blood, [which paid the penalty for our sin and resulted in] the forgiveness and complete pardon of our sin, in accordance with the riches of His grace which He lavished on us. In all wisdom and understanding [with practical insight] He made known to us the mystery of His will according to His good pleasure, which He purposed in Christ, with regard to the fulfillment of the times [that is, the end of history, the climax of the ages]—to bring all things together in Christ, [both] things in the heavens and things on the earth.

2 Corinthians 5:21 AMP

He made Christ who knew no sin to [judicially] be sin on our behalf, so that in Him we would become the righteousness of God [that is, we would be made acceptable to Him and placed in a right relationship with Him by His gracious lovingkindness].

Romans 5:8 NKJV

But God demonstrates His own love toward us, in that while we were still sinners, Christ died for us.

John 1:17 AMP

For the Law was given through Moses, but grace [the unearned, undeserved favor of God] and truth came through Jesus Christ.

Hebrews 2:14-15 BSB

Now since the children have flesh and blood, He too shared in their humanity, so that by His death He might destroy him who holds the power of death, that is, the devil, and free those who all their lives were held in slavery by their fear of death.

John 10:10 NKJV

The thief does not come except to steal, and to kill, and to destroy. I have come that they may have life, and that they may have it more abundantly.

Romans 10:13 KJV

For whosoever shall call upon the name of the Lord shall be saved.

Psalm 68:20 AMP

God is to us a God of acts of salvation; And to God the Lord belong escapes from death [setting us free].

John 3:16-17 KJV

For God so loved the world, that he gave his only begotten Son, that whosoever believeth in him should not perish, but have everlasting life. For God sent not his Son into the world to condemn the world; but that the world through him might be saved.

Isaiah 55:12 NKJV

For you shall go out with joy, and be led out with peace; The mountains and the hills shall break forth into singing before you, and all the trees of the field shall clap their hands.

Acts 2:21 NKJV

And it shall come to pass that whoever calls on the name of the Lord shall be saved.

Romans 5:21 NLT

So just as sin ruled over all people and brought them to death, now God's wonderful grace rules instead, giving us right standing with God and resulting in eternal life through Jesus Christ our Lord.

Exodus 15:13 BSB

With loving devotion You will lead the people You have redeemed; with Your strength You will guide them to Your holy dwelling.

Romans 4:24-25 AMP

But for our sake also—to whom righteousness will be credited, as those who believe in Him who raised Jesus our Lord from the dead—who was betrayed and crucified because of our sins, and was raised [from the dead] because of our justification [our acquittal—absolving us of all sin before God].

Philippians 3:20-21 AMP

But [we are different, because] our citizenship is in heaven. And from there we eagerly await [the coming of] the Savior, the Lord Jesus Christ; who, by exerting that power which enables Him even to subject everything to Himself, will [not only] transform [but completely refashion] our earthly bodies so that they will be like His glorious resurrected body.

Colossians 1:12-13 BSB

Giving thanks to the Father, who has qualified you to share in the inheritance of the saints in the light. He has rescued us from the dominion of darkness and brought us into the kingdom of His beloved Son,

Hebrews 2:17 NIV

For this reason he had to be made like them, fully human in every way, in order that he might become a merciful and faithful high priest in service to God, and that he might make atonement for the sins of the people.

Hebrews 9:24, 26 ESV

For Christ has entered, not into holy places made with hands, which are copies of the true things, but into heaven itself, now to appear in the presence of God on our behalf. ...for then he would have had to suffer repeatedly since the foundation of the world. But as it is, he has appeared once for all at the end of the ages to put away sin by the sacrifice of himself.

1 Peter 1:18-19 NKJV

Knowing that you were not redeemed with corruptible things, like silver or gold, from your aimless conduct received by tradition from your fathers, but with the precious blood of Christ, as of a lamb without blemish and without spot.

1 Peter 3:18 AMP

For indeed Christ died for sins once for all, the Just and Righteous for the unjust and unrighteous [the Innocent for the guilty] so that He might bring us to God, having been put to death in the flesh, but made alive in the Spirit.

John 3:14-18 BSB

Just as Moses lifted up the snake in the wilderness, so the Son of Man must be lifted up, that everyone who believes in Him may have eternal life. For God so loved the world that He gave His one and only Son, that everyone who believes in Him shall not perish but have eternal life. For God did not send His Son into the world to condemn the world, but to save the world through Him. Whoever believes in Him is not condemned, but whoever does not believe has already been condemned, because he has not believed in the name of God's one and only Son.

John 3:36 NKJV

He who believes in the Son has everlasting life; and he who does not believe the Son shall not see life, but the wrath of God abides on him.

CHARIS
BIBLE COLLEGE

God has more for you.

Are you longing to find your God-given purpose? At Charis Bible College you will establish a firm foundation in the Word of God and receive hands-on ministry experience to **find, follow** and **fulfill** your purpose.

Scan the QR code to visit CharisBibleCollege.org

Admissions@awmcharis.com
(844) 360-9577

Change your life. **Change the world.**

life FOUNDATIONS
with Carrie Pickett

Join Carrie as she uncovers the foundational principles of the Word of God and discover how these truths can transform your everyday life.

Scan the QR code to watch full episodes of Life Foundations

CONTACT INFORMATION

Charis Bible College

800 Gospel Truth Way

Woodland Park, CO 80863

info@charisbiblecollege.org

Helpline Available 24/7: 719-635-1111

CharisBibleCollege.org

Also visit Carrie at CarriePickett.com